CONTENTS

🦶 Watch out for the *Sign of the Foot*! Whenever you see this sign in the book it means there are some more details at the *FOOT* of the page. Like here.

BEFORE WE BEGIN

ONE SPRING MORNING

Two men with spiky blond hair are sitting on the white cliffs of Dover. If you walk

up behind them slowly, you might mistake their heads for two hedgehogs which have settled down to look at the view. The two men are Ancient Britons . They gaze out to sea.

It's a fine spring morning. The waves sparkle beneath them. Behind them, the country is green, rich and fertile. AD 43 is a great time to be alive - or at least it should be ...

Ancient Briton is a term usually used to describe someone who lived in Britain in prehistoric times, that is, when people didn't yet read and write.

5

ROME ON THE ROAM

The Empire made easy

Unfortunately for the Ancient Britons, in AD 43 the mighty Emperor Tiberius Claudius Drusus Nero Germanicus (10 BC - AD 54), or *Claudius* for short, had ordered a vast army of Roman soldiers to invade Britain.

Hi Claudius!

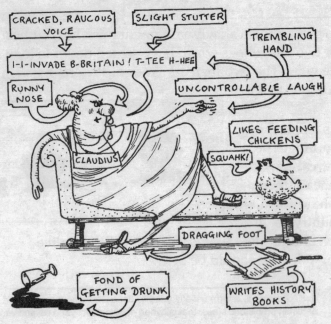

CRACKED, RAUCOUS VOICE

SLIGHT STUTTER

TREMBLING HAND

I-I-INVADE B-BRITAIN! T-TEE H-HEE

RUNNY NOSE

UNCONTROLLABLE LAUGH

CLAUDIUS

LIKES FEEDING CHICKENS

SQUAHK!

DRAGGING FOOT

FOND OF GETTING DRUNK

WRITES HISTORY BOOKS

WHY CLAUDIUS?

Claudius became Emperor of Rome after the murder of his mad nephew, the Emperor Caligula, just after one o'clock on 24th January AD 41. Caligula's killers, their swords still bloody, saw Claudius' slippers sticking out from beneath a curtain where he was hiding. They decided to make him Emperor because they couldn't find anybody else suitable - Claudius would do because he was a member of the Roman ruling family.

THOUGHT YOU'D SLIP AWAY DID YOU?

At that time the Roman Empire was the mightiest empire the world has ever seen, so Claudius had become the most powerful man in the world - even though he was a drunkard, whom most people thought was weak in the head!

Claudius needed a war and a victory in order to prove to the Roman people what a good emperor he could be. That's why he ordered the invasion of Britain.

The Roman Empire in AD 43

The Romans were ruthlessly efficient and they were brilliant soldiers. They built an army which was the best in the world for more than a thousand years. And with that army they conquered an empire which lasted in the west until AD 476. (In the east the *Byzantine* Empire or Eastern Roman Empire continued until AD 1453 when it was finally overrun by the Turks.)

Searching for Clues

The Roman Empire soared like a comet for hundreds of years and then fell like a stone. Britain was part of that Empire and part of the fall. Since it all happened an incredibly long time ago, you might expect that

This is about the same as the population of modern Birmingham.

nothing much would be left to tell us what went on. Well, a lot has disappeared, but the Empire was so big and it went on for such a long time that there are still plenty of clues as to what the Ancient Romans were like and how they lived:

 Many of their books have survived in old libraries. We know the names of their famous writers, some of whom wrote about the British

and their battles with the Romans, and we can read about Roman generals and emperors.

 They built to last. The countries they once ruled are littered with the vast remains of theatres, temples, aqueducts and even whole cities.

Aqueducts are artificial channels which carry water above the ground, sometimes for long distances.

There are over a million Roman inscriptions which can still be read on old gravestones and monuments.

 Archaeologists  dig up the remains of everyday objects, such as old pots or hair combs. These help us to understand how the Romans used to live.

THAT'S ALL OF US AULUS

Following Claudius' orders, in AD 43 Aulus Plautius, the Roman commander in Gaul (modern France), had gathered an army of forty thousand men, plus some elephants to impress the natives, at Gesoriacum (the modern French port of Boulogne). He was to invade Britain as soon as possible.

This would not be the first Roman invasion of Britain. In 55-56 BC, nearly a hundred years before, the Britons had been beaten by the famous Roman general Julius Caesar. But Caesar had to return to Rome for political reasons before his conquest of Britain was complete.

Archaeologists are historians who look for clues about the past by searching for buried remains.

After Caesar's troops had left, the Britons had gone back to their 'savage' Celtic ways, as the Romans saw them. In fact by AD 43 the Britons were helping rebellious Gauls to fight the Romans, egged on by Druids who were based in Britain. Plautius and his Emperor Claudius knew that they had to beat the Britons if there was to be peace in Gaul.

In other words, they were going to teach those pesky Britons a lesson. No wonder the two Ancient Britons were sitting on the white cliffs of Dover; they were looking for the sails of the Roman invasion fleet.

They wouldn't have long to wait.

Druids were the priests of the Ancient Britons and Gauls. More on them later.

BARMY BRITONS

BRITAIN BEFORE THE ROMANS

MUD IN BRITAIN

In AD 43, Britain was divided into a crazy patchwork of tribal kingdoms ruled by small-time royalty. The aristocracy tended to live in hill-forts with high earth walls, probably topped with wooden fences. You can still see the remains of these hill-forts on the tops of many hills today.

WHICH TRIBE DO YOU BELONG TO?
If you had been alive in AD 43, which tribe would have ruled over the region where you live today?

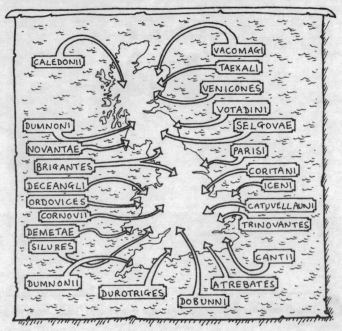

Whether inside the walls of the hill-forts or out in the country, people lived in circular huts made of mud daubed over sticks and twigs . The country was wild and wooded. There were massive areas of thick forest where bears and wolves roamed freely. Between the forests the people were mostly farmers who worked small fields around their farms.

Actually the Ancient Britons weren't total savages, they did produce some goods to sell. Merchants from the civilizations of the Mediterranean had been sailing to south-west England since the time of the Ancient Greeks, at least four hundred years before, to barter for tin, leather, slaves and other goods.

This mixture of mud and sticks is called *wattle and daub*.

These goods were exchanged for luxury items, such as wine and decorated bowls. The Ancient Britons were very fond of wine and valued it highly. Aristocrats would sometimes exchange a healthy slave for a single *amphora* .

DINNER DANGERS!

The Ancient Britons were *Celts*, as were many of the people of northern Europe. Early Celts spoke *Celtic* and liked head hunting and human sacrifice. (The doors of the early Celts were hung with the heads of their enemies). Even in Roman times they would sacrifice a child before any major battle in order to foresee the future. The child would be cut open and any unusual features of the *entrails*, or insides, would be regarded as clues to understanding the future. The Romans did the same sort of thing but only with animals.

HMM. THE LIVER'S HEALTHY. PERHAPS WE'LL _LIVE_ TO FIGHT ANOTHER DAY!

 An *amphora* was a large earthenware jar used for storing and carrying liquids and other goods.

Above all, the Celts loved fighting and fought each other at the slightest opportunity. At their feasts the thigh bone was always given to the bravest hero. Warriors would sometimes fight to the death over drumsticks!

Celts were described by the Romans as being large and fierce with blond hair . They probably looked much like the majority of people of modern England - although you might not want to ask one to dinner!

The modern Irish and Welsh describe themselves as Celtic, but they look a lot different to the Celts who lived in England when the Romans invaded. In fact early Irish aristocrats often dyed their hair blond to fit the fashionable Celtic image of that time.

COMPARE THE HAIR

CELTIC WARRIOR

NO HELMET, SO AS NOT TO SPOIL THE HAIR-DO

FIERCE EYES

DEEP, HARSH-SOUNDING VOICE

LONG MOUSTACHE

SOMETIMES FOUGHT NAKED TO SHOW CONTEMPT FOR DANGER

BODY SHAVEN, APART FROM HEAD AND UPPER LIP

SLENDER – ANY YOUNG MAN WHO GREW TOO FAT COULD BE FINED

CELTIC LADY

EYEBROWS DYED BLACK WITH BERRY JUICE

LONG FAIR HAIR – DYED IF NECESSARY – DESCRIBED BY ONE ROMAN WRITER AS A 'STREAMING MANE'

CHEEKS REDDENED WITH A HERB CALLED RUAM

STRONG WHITE ARMS. THE WOMEN WERE DESCRIBED BY SICULUS, A ROMAN WRITER, AS STRONGER THAN THE MEN, AND FOND OF QUARRELLING

HARSH VOICE

Roman writers tended to exaggerate about the Celts.

16

Roman Gentleman

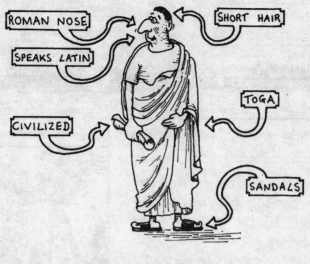

ROMAN NOSE

SHORT HAIR

SPEAKS LATIN

TOGA

CIVILIZED

SANDALS

Roman Lady

ROMAN NOSE

FANCY HAIR-DO

JEWELLERY

SPEAKS LATIN

STOLA

SANDALS

CLAUDIUS MAKES HIS MOVE

AD 43, Aulus Plautius sets sail from Boulogne with an army of 40,000 men.

They land on the south coast of England and fight a two-day battle against the defending Celts. The Celtic chariots  are no match for the disciplined Roman legions.

The Roman army marches north and the British tribes give way before them, taking their belongings and herds of animals with them.

War chariots were made of wickerwork and drawn by two ponies. The charioteer drove the chariot to the thick of the battle, then the warrior jumped out and fought on foot.

The Romans capture Camulodunum (modern Colchester), the largest British town at that time. Caratacus and Togodumnus, the wild sons of the powerful British king Cunobelin - now dead - govern Camulodunum. These two young men are the leaders of British resistance to Rome. Togodumnus will not live much longer.

Claudius enters Camulodunum in triumph, while Roman armies fan out across the land.

Caratacus the young British leader flees to take up the fight elsewhere.

A TALE OF TWO Cs

Caratacus

The British leader Caratacus escaped into Wales. He kept on fighting bravely until the Romans defeated him and took his wife and children prisoner. Then Caratacus took refuge in the kingdom of the Brigantes in the north of England which was still free of Roman rule. The Brigantes were a primitive tribe of nomads who tended large herds of cattle. They bred the best chariot ponies in Britain and they hated the Romans as much as anybody.

Cartimandua

Cartimandua 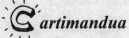 was queen of the Brigantes. Unlike many of her people, she was friendly towards the Romans, or at least she didn't want to offend them by giving refuge to their main enemy, Caratacus.

In AD 51 Cartimandua handed Caratacus over to the Roman governor of Britain. Caratacus was taken in chains to Rome.

Her name meant 'Sleek Filly'.

TRIUMPH!

When he ordered the invasion of Britain, Claudius didn't just want to teach the Britons a lesson. He was after a really big *triumph* to impress the people back in Rome. A triumph wasn't just a victory in the sense of the word today. It was a glittering parade through the streets of Rome and it was only granted to the victors of specially important battles. Claudius needed a major triumph to prove that he was a hero, not just a middle-aged man with a stammer who had been found hiding behind a curtain.

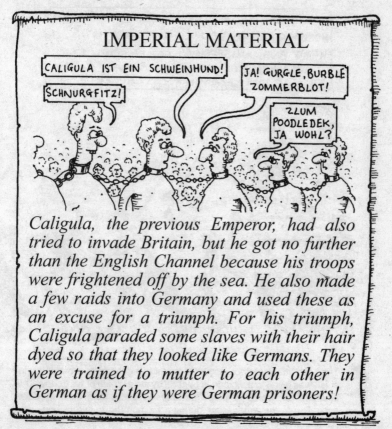

IMPERIAL MATERIAL

CALIGULA IST EIN SCHWEINHUND!

SCHNURGFITZ!

JA! GURGLE, BURBLE ZOMMERBLOT!

ZLUM POODLEDEK, JA WOHL?

Caligula, the previous Emperor, had also tried to invade Britain, but he got no further than the English Channel because his troops were frightened off by the sea. He also made a few raids into Germany and used these as an excuse for a triumph. For his triumph, Caligula paraded some slaves with their hair dyed so that they looked like Germans. They were trained to mutter to each other in German as if they were German prisoners!

In a triumphal procession, magistrates and senators walked at the head, followed by white oxen for sacrifice and wagons loaded with booty taken from the enemy. Next came the prisoners of war, some carried shoulder high on platforms, ready for execution or slavery. The general , in this case Claudius, rode in a gilded chariot, wearing a laurel wreath and carrying a sceptre and an olive branch, the symbol of peace and plenty. Last came the soldiers carrying sticks instead of swords. When it was all over they were given a huge feast and a present of money.

A SLAVE STOOD AT THE GENERAL'S SHOULDER, HOLDING A GOLDEN CROWN OVER HIS HEAD AND WHISPERING CONTINUOUSLY, 'REMEMBER YOU ARE JUST A MAN' SO AS TO STOP HIM BECOMING CONCEITED.

The Latin title *imperator*, originally meaning a general or commander-in-chief, was given to a victorious general by the acclaim of his troops. This is where our words *emperor* and *imperial* come from. In early days, according to the writer Pliny, during a triumph the general's body was painted bright red.

The procession wound its way through the streets of Rome, finally arriving at the temple of Jupiter Optimus, greatest of the Roman gods, where the general offered up the laurel wreath of victory and the white oxen were sacrificed.

Claudius had had his triumph by the time Caratacus was handed over. But Caratacus was put on show in a sort of mini-triumph. He made such a good speech

that Claudius spared him from execution. Caratacus is said to have died in Rome in AD 54.

BOOT CAMPS

- OR SHOULD WE SAY SANDAL CAMPS?
THE ROMAN ARMY

POWER PLAY

HOW DID THE ROMANS BUILD THEIR MIGHTY EMPIRE?

WITH THE SWORD!

Roman armies were the best armies in the world for nearly a thousand years and no one had a chance against them. Their soldiers were well trained and well disciplined and their weapons were just right for the types of battles they had to fight. Barbarians went down like daisies under a lawnmower.

During the height of the Empire, the Roman armies usually totalled around 400,000 men. The soldiers could march or jog quickly to any trouble spot along well-built roads. 400,000 was enough to control their 45 million subjects and to deal with troublesome barbarians outside their borders, such as the Ancient Britons.

FELIX THE FOOT SOLDIER

Foot soldiers were the core of the army. There were four types: the *hastati* and *princeps* were young men in the prime of life, the *velites* were light skirmishers and the *triarii* were old-timers ◄, looking forward to retirement and marriage after their twenty-five years of service. (Until AD 197 Roman soldiers were not allowed to marry.)

LEGIONNAIRE AROUND AD 50

BRONZE HELMET

FLEXIBLE PLATE ARMOUR

OVER THE AGE OF EIGHTEEN, AND OVER 1·65 METRES TALL

TWO JAVELINS OR 'PILA', ONE LIGHT, ONE HEAVY

SHORT 'SPANISH' SWORD

RECTANGULAR PLYWOOD SHIELD

Triarii fought at the back. The Roman saying 'the battle went to the triarii' meant a desperate situation.

The typical Roman sword was copied from a style first used in Spain.

BOOT CAMP

Each soldier was as fit as a fiddle and an expert fighter. They had to practise hard:

Thirty kilometre march with full kit three times a month

General training in stone-slinging, swimming and riding

Sword practice with wooden swords

Long jump and high jump

Vaulting in full armour

Drill once a day (twice during initial training)

When the time came for a battle, the standard tactic was to advance to about twenty metres from the enemy, keeping a space of two metres between each soldier. Then the soldiers would throw their lighter javelins followed by the heavier. The javelins often stuck in the enemies' shields. They had a barbed point which was difficult to pull out, and the metal shaft below the tip was thin so that it bent on impact, making it useless to throw back.

Close up, the soldiers went to work with their swords, frequently dropping to one knee and holding their shields above them while striking upwards. Great big Celts with long swords used to find this technique difficult to fight against.

Ancient battles were incredibly bloody affairs. Imagine a slaughter of say eighty thousand men (the number is nothing out of the ordinary) as happened at the defeat of one British army, all killed by stabbing or slashing 🖌. An adult man has about five litres of blood. That makes up to 400,000 litres of blood swashing around on the battlefield - enough to fill a fair sized lake!

During the revolt of Boudicca. More of that later.

GOING BALLISTIC

Not all fighting was hand to hand. The Romans had long distance weapons as well. Specially useful were two types of catapult:

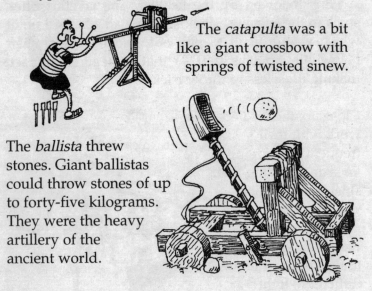

The *catapulta* was a bit like a giant crossbow with springs of twisted sinew.

The *ballista* threw stones. Giant ballistas could throw stones of up to forty-five kilograms. They were the heavy artillery of the ancient world.

FOLLOW THE EAGLE!

The soldiers were organised into units of about eighty men, called *centuries* 👣. Six centuries made a *cohort* and ten cohorts together with about 120 despatch riders made a *legion*. At the height of the Empire there were twenty-eight Roman legions and the rest of the army was recruited from *auxiliary* forces made up of men from other nations. Normal battle array was two Roman legions in the centre, flanked by two auxiliary legions, with horse soldiers, or *cavalry*, on the wings.

It is commonly thought that centuries originally contained a hundred soldiers. The Latin word *centum* means a hundred.

OFFICER MATERIAL

Tribunes were aristocratic staff officers, often not very experienced.

The *Legatus* was the commander of a legion.

Centurions commanded centuries.

HANDLE FOR PULLING STANDARD OUT OF THE GROUND

The eagle was the standard of the legion. Loss of the eagle to an enemy was a major disgrace. It was carried by an officer called an *aquilifer.*

As well as officers, legions needed scouts, despatch riders, catapult makers, water engineers, medical orderlies and a master builder.

DO AS YOU'RE TOLD OR ELSE!

Centurions were assisted by standard bearers, trumpeters and a *tessarius*, an officer who received the camp password at night. Long-serving centurions were the backbone of the army. Many spent more than forty years in the service 👣 , but they were often brutal and corrupt. They carried a vine cane to keep discipline.

I'LL DECIMATE YOU!

Discipline was strict. Deserters and sentries who left their posts were executed. There were even generals who executed their own sons for disobedience. But *decimation* 👣 was the worst punishment. During a decimation, every tenth man of an offending cohort was clubbed or stoned to death by the men of another cohort. The rest of the decimated cohort had to eat only barley and might have to sleep outside the camp at night for the period of their disgrace.

👣 One centurion is recorded as having spent sixty-one years in the army.

👣 *Decimus* is Latin for tenth.

TIME TO MOVE

Roman soldiers had to carry all their own vital supplies - no wonder they were known as 'Marius' mules', after the famous general who first made them carry their own baggage around 106 BC.

There was a real mule for every eight men. The mule carried their shared tent and any surplus items. In hostile territory the legions marched in battle order with their baggage mules and other equipment protected between the columns of soldiers.

LET'S GO CAMPING

There were no ready-made campsites for Roman soldiers, no shower facilities and no camper vans. Having marched perhaps thirty kilometres, or even as many as fifty, the tired soldiers were not allowed to rest until they had built a fortified camp.

Half the army dug a square ditch and mud rampart, while the other half stood guard in battle array. The fence posts they had carried with them were hammered into the top of the rampart and joined with links of chain. Then after the positions of the various tents had been marked out, the baggage train was led into the fortified area and the legion could start to relax. Camps were always laid out in exactly the same way so there was never any danger of getting lost.

There were no gates on temporary camps. But permanent camps not only had gates, they had stone walls and some, the legionary bases, stayed in the same place for hundreds of years. Several English towns such as Chester and Cirencester grew up around Roman camps.

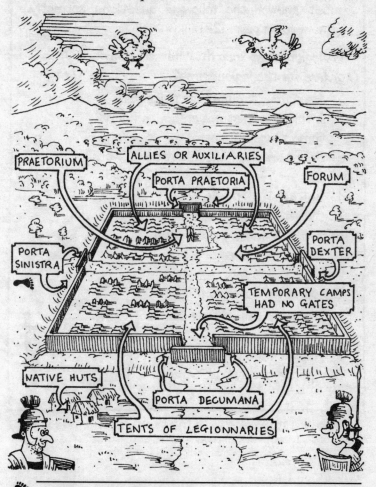

PRAETORIUM

ALLIES OR AUXILIARIES

PORTA PRAETORIA

FORUM

PORTA SINISTRA

PORTA DEXTER

TEMPORARY CAMPS HAD NO GATES

NATIVE HUTS

PORTA DECUMANA

TENTS OF LEGIONNARIES

Porta means gate in latin. *Sinister* means left and *dexter* means right. The *praetorium* was the camp heaquarters, so the *porta praetoria* was the gate of the headquarters. The *porta decumana* was the main gate.

STRAP UP YOUR SANDALS

COULD *YOU* BE A ROMAN? (PART I)

You are applying for a job as Roman general. You must answer the following questions correctly. (Answers on page 122)

1 A legion must keep fit. What are your orders for the legionnaires?

a   A sauna with massage twice daily
b   A thirty kilometre march with full kit three times a month
c   Sword practice with sharpened swords

2 What are the triarii?

a   Old soldiers who fight at the back
b   Soldiers who try extra hard
c   Three-pointed spears

3 How large is a legion?

a   3 metres tall and about five round the middle
b   Approximately 400 men
c   Approximately 5,000 men

THEY CAME, THEY SAW, THEY TOOK

ROADS, WALLS AND THINGS IN BETWEEN

> Having conquered half of England, we Romans were ready to enjoy it.

TIME FOR A BREATHER

The Romans lost no time in rebuilding Camulodunum (Colchester), the largest Celtic town in Britain, as a town for retired legionnaires. Such towns were called *colonies*. Soon there was a massive temple to the Emperor Claudius just outside the town boundaries.

Britain in AD 60

BRIGANTES – FAIRLY FRIENDLY TO ROME

BARBARIANS

COLCHESTER (CAMULODUNUM)

ST. ALBANS (VERULAMIUM)

UNDER ROMAN CONTROL

LONDON

And it was all paid for by taxes from local people.

Everything was going brilliantly for the Romans, apart from a few problems with troublesome Celts in the north and in Wales. The governor withdrew most of the legions from southern England.

Roman emperors were worshipped as gods. More about that later.

Roman mistake No.1 - destroying the Druids

The Druids had many strange and frightening rituals. They made sacrifices in groves of sacred trees, where every tree was 'sprinkled with human gore', according to descriptions by the Roman writer Tacitus. They are said to have built huge hollow figures of men out of sticks then crammed these 'wicker men' full of human prisoners before setting fire to them. They cut magic mistletoe with golden sickles and even ate deadly nightshade  to give themselves visions. And they disapproved of reading and writing, which is why we know so little about them.

The headquarters of all the Druids in Europe was on the island of Anglesey off the north coast of Wales. Safe on their island they continued their sacred rituals.

Romans thought the Druids were disgusting. What they found really disgusting was that the Druids encouraged people to fight the Romans.

Being Romans, the Romans set out to crush the Druids. They attacked Anglesey.

Deadly nightshade is an extremely poisonous plant. The berries will often kill whoever eats them.

We have a description of the scene before the battle by a Roman general later to become Emperor Agricola:

'The enemy lined the shore in a dense armed mass. Among them black-robed women with dishevelled hair like furies, brandishing torches. Close by stood Druids raising their hands to heaven and screaming dreadful curses. This weird sight awed the Romans into a kind of paralysis ...'

But not for long. The Romans attacked and won. They chopped down the sacred groves and slaughtered the Britons. Then almost at the moment of victory their commander, the governor Suetonius Paulinus, received a message of far worse trouble in the south ...

ROMAN MISTAKE No.2 (A BIG MISTAKE) - BUGGING BOUDICCA

Boudicca, Queen of the Iceni, was a huge woman with a harsh voice and a mass of red hair which fell to her knees. She was terrifying, and she despised Roman men 'if these can indeed be called men who bathe in warm water, eat delicacies ... and sleep on soft couches'. Unfortunately for everyone it seems that the Romans didn't notice her attitude.

37

When Boudicca's husband King Prasutagus died in AD 59 or 60, the Romans beat Boudicca and tried to take her kingdom from her. Boudicca was not the sort of woman to accept this treatment meekly. She started a mass rebellion of British warriors.

The Romans were caught on the hop because their army was in Anglesey dealing with the Druids. By the time the legions had marched south again, Boudicca's followers had sacked Colchester, London and St Albans, taking no prisoners, selling no slaves and killing up to seventy thousand Romans. There is still a layer of ash beneath the streets of the City of London from the time of Boudicca's attack.

The main Roman legions hurried south in forced marches along a newly-built road known as Watling Street . They were too late to stop the destruction but they finally defeated Boudicca in a battle in the Midlands . The British had brought their wives and children to watch the battle from a sort of wagon park behind their main army. But there was nothing to watch except slaughter. About eighty thousand tribesmen and four hundred Romans lost their lives. Boudicca escaped but probably poisoned herself soon afterwards. Thus ended the largest ever British rebellion against the Romans.

POISON

The modern A5 follows the route of Watling Street.

The battlefield was probably at Mancetter (near Atherston) on the A5, where there is now a stone quarry.

LOADS OF ROADS

Boudicca was beaten by Roman roads almost as much as by Roman soldiers. It was the roads which allowed Suetonius Paulinus to gather his forces quickly for the counter-attack.

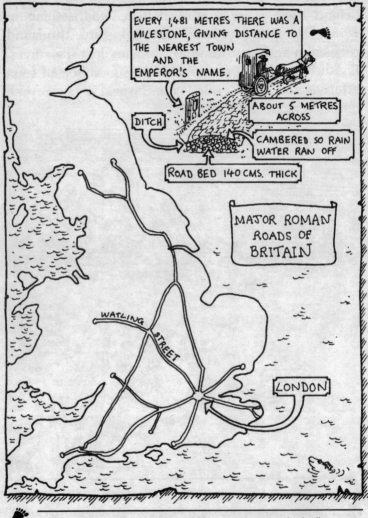

EVERY 1,481 METRES THERE WAS A MILESTONE, GIVING DISTANCE TO THE NEAREST TOWN AND THE EMPEROR'S NAME.

DITCH

ABOUT 5 METRES ACROSS

CAMBERED SO RAIN WATER RAN OFF

ROAD BED 140 CMS. THICK

MAJOR ROMAN ROADS OF BRITAIN

WATLING STREET

LONDON

1,481 metres is a Roman mile, 1,609 metres is a standard mile.

The first Roman roads in Britain would have been made quickly and would not have lasted long in British weather, but they were soon replaced by roads which were seriously Roman and seriously permanent. An average Roman road contained 20,000 tonnes of stone per mile. They were mainly built by the army, but slaves and prisoners helped them - about 40,000 British prisoners of war were forced to build roads in neighbouring Gaul.

Roads were laid out using special surveying instruments and smoke beacons. They tended to be laid in straight lines with major changes of direction at high points from which the surveyors could see the next smoke beacon and aim for it.

85,000 kilometres of roads criss-crossed the Empire. There was a saying: 'All roads lead to Rome' which in a sense they all did, since that's where all the orders came from. Imperial messengers could travel at speed on relays of horses kept at intervals of ten to twenty kilometres, carrying the Emperor's edicts to the furthest corners of his empire - such as Britain.

TALL WALLS

In the north of Britain the roads fizzled out. The Romans never conquered all of Scotland. It was full of savages, and anyway there was nothing there worth grabbing.

Instead they built a wall to keep the savages out. It's called Hadrian's Wall after the emperor who ordered it built and you can still see bits of it. It was the largest structure ever built by the Romans, which is saying quite a lot. It took ten years to build .

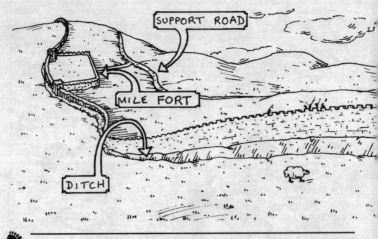

In AD 142, another wall, called the Antonine Wall, was built in Scotland, between the Firths of Forth and Clyde, but it was abandoned in AD 196. It was ordered by the emperor Antoninus Pius.

Hadrian's Wall stretched 120 kilometres from Bowness in the west to Wallsend in the east, right across the north of England. It was wide enough for a chariot to ride on top of it, and along its length were sixteen large forts with smaller forts every Roman mile, together with signalling turrets. There was a hospital in every fortress and in most of the forts.

The wall was manned by soldiers from all over the Empire. We know this from tombstones and other objects which they left behind. For instance, some cavalry from Germany known as 'Notfrieds Irregulars' were stationed at Housesteads  in the centre of the wall and a unit of Africans was stationed at Burgh-by-Sands in the west. The soldiers did a good job. In all the time the wall was in use (from AD 122-383) it was only once overrun.

Roman name *Borocovicium*.

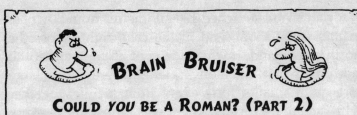
Could you be a Roman? (part 2)

Romans used letters for numbers: I = 1, V = 5, X = 10, L = 50, C = 100, D = 500, M = 1000. The numbers in between were made up of two or more of these letters. These were normally added together. For instance III = 3, VI = 6, XVI = 16. However, if a number was smaller than the one immediately after it, it was subtracted from that number, e.g. IV = 4, IXX = 19, XLIV = 44.

The following are the Roman numbers from 1 to 20: I, II, III, IV, V VI, VII, VIII, IX, X, XI, XII, XIII, XIV, XV, XVI, XVII, XVIII, IXX, XX

Can you work out what these numbers are? (Answers on page 122.)

a XXIII
b XLVII
c CLXXIV

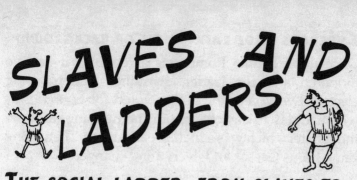

SLAVES AND LADDERS

THE SOCIAL LADDER, FROM SLAVES TO EMPERORS WITH RUNGS IN BETWEEN

For nearly four hundred years Britain was a small province on the edge of a mighty empire. The governors who ruled it were appointed by the Emperor in Rome and society was organised along Roman lines.

POWER PYRAMID

GOVERNORS AND OTHER TOP OFFICIALS (USUALLY ROMAN NOBLES)

EMPEROR

KNIGHTS

FREEDMEN

SLAVES

Once upon a time Rome was a republic: it had no monarch and the leader, or rather leaders, were elected. Every year the nobles voted for two *consuls* who had day to day charge of running things and ran the senate, which was a bit like parliament. Then along came Julius Caesar and everything changed.

'Caesar' meant 'head of hair', which is strange because both Julius and Augustus, the next 'Caesar' (as all the emperors came to be called), were bald. Julius took all power in Rome into his own hands. From that time on Rome was always ruled by one or two powerful men who came to be given titles such as *Caesar, Augustus* and *Imperator*, meaning emperor, by the senate. Julius was stabbed to death on the Ides 🐾 of March (15 March) 44 BC by a bunch of conspirators who thought he had grown too powerful.

🐾 The Romans counted dates from three fixed points in each month: *Kalends, Nones* and *Ides*, so a day was said to be so many days before or after one of these fixed days or actually on a fixed day.

GREAT DATES

Julius changed the Roman world, and he also changed the calendar. The old Roman calendar had only ten months with a period in winter without any months, March being the first month of the year. (The extra months of January and February were added later, which is why September, which comes from the Latin word *septum* meaning 'seventh' is now the ninth month.) The months were too short, so that each year started earlier than the year before. Julius sorted things out. The months of the year as we know them today are almost the same as on Julius' Roman calendar.

January - called after Janus, god of beginnings and doorways among other things
February - after a Roman feast of purification
March - the first month of the year until 153 BC, after Mars, god of war and originally agriculture
April - probably after Aphrodite, Greek goddess of love
May - called after the Roman goddess Maia
June - means sacred to the goddess Juno
July - called after Julius Caesar, used to be called Quintilis - the fifth month (from mid-March)
August - called after the Emperor Augustus, used to be called Sextilis - the sixth month
September - the seventh month
October - from the Latin *octo* meaning eight
November - from the Latin *novem* meaning nine
December - from the Latin *decem* meaning ten

CLEOPATRA
A CLASSY ACT

In 48 BC Queen Cleopatra of Egypt was eighteen years old. At that time Caesar had come to Egypt with a large army to defeat another powerful Roman called Pompey. Cleopatra had herself wrapped up in a carpet and smuggled into Caesar's presence. Almost as soon as he saw her, Caesar fell in love with her and soon took her to Rome.

After Caesar's murder, Cleopatra and Caesar's young friend, Marcus Antonius, also fell madly in love. Unfortunately, Antony and Cleopatra were defeated in a civil war by the next Emperor, a short, balding young man called Octavianus, later called Augustus, who was Caesar's heir. Captured by Octavianus, Cleopatra tried to charm him as well but failed.

She killed herself with a bite from a poisonous snake called an asp. She already knew about asps from experiments on live human beings.

LET'S TRY AN ASP ON THIS ONE.

ON YOUR GUARD!

Each emperor was protected by a special regiment of several thousand soldiers known as the *Praetorian Guard*. They were paid three-and-a-half times as much as ordinary legionnaires, wore a special old-fashioned uniform and were the only soldiers permanently stationed in Rome.

Praetorians were meant to protect emperors, but they often killed them instead. When new emperors came to power, they used to give the Praetorians a special bonus worth up to five years' pay - really a bribe to keep them sweet. No bribe could mean no emperor - and often did! It was officers of the Praetorian Guard who murdered Caligula, the mad emperor who ruled before Claudius.

POSH TOFFS AND POOR PLEBS

Top of the Roman toffs were the *patricians*. Usually the governor of Britain was a patrician appointed by the emperor. They were aristocrats. They sat in the Senate, lived in beautiful houses in Rome and often thought themselves superior to the emperor himself, who in later years was often not an aristocrat.

All other Romans were known as *plebeians* or *plebs* for short. In the early years of Rome they had no rights and were forbidden to marry patricians or to hold important jobs. Later they got their own assembly led by *tribunes* and won the right to hold important jobs. Eventually it was impossible to tell a patrician from a rich pleb.

Knights were rich plebs and became a separate middle class. The second most important man in Britain after the governor was the *procurator* who was always a knight. He looked after tax collection and the emperor's mines and estates.

NERO
A MAD EMPEROR STORY

Nero (AD 37-68) didn't like Britain. He thought it was cold and wet. (The fact that Boudicca's rebellion happened during his reign can't have helped.)

He also didn't like his mother. Having decided to get rid of her, he persuaded Mum to board a special boat during a parade of ships. Little did Mum know that the boat was specially designed to let in water and its roof was designed to lower as the water rushed in, thus crushing those inside. Unfortunately Nero's evil scheme backfired. Mum escaped and swam to safety in front of a large crowd.

Nero had to have her murdered by a soldier instead.

SLAVE GRADES

Slaves were bottom of the heap in Roman Britain. They were the property of their owners who could do what they wanted with them. However, some slaves had quite important jobs. The first British civil servant whose name we know was a slave named Anencletus . He worked for the London city council's staff, perhaps as a secretary.

In fact nearly all work in the Roman Empire was done by slaves. Slaves worked the farms and mines, there were slave doctors and dentists and secretaries like Anencletus. Slave labour became a habit: in Rome itself none of the free citizens were prepared to labour . They were supported by supplies of food and drink given out by the government and the produce of their slaves if they owned any.

Anencletus is Greek for 'blameless'.

In the later years of the Empire there was six months' holiday per year anyway. But not for slaves!

WAVES OF SLAVES

With each new conquest, more slaves flooded on to the Roman slave markets. After the Romans conquered Sardinia there was such a glut of Sardinian slaves that 'cheap as a Sardinian' became a common saying. An ordinary slave was cheaper than a horse or even a cow. You could pick them up for 500 denarii - a horse would cost you much more. In the slave market on the Greek island of Delos, ten thousand slaves might be sold on the same day. There would have been thousands of British slaves of both sexes for sale after the Roman invasion. Later, when the conquests stopped, the supply of new slaves dried up and they became more expensive.

The number of slaves was a constant worry to the government. In Italy there were three slaves to every free person. In Britain the number of slaves compared to freemen would have been less, but even so there would have been a great many. Slaves weren't allowed to wear uniforms in case they saw how they outnumbered the free people and then rebelled.

SPARTACUS
A SAD STORY

Spartacus was a deserter from the army who was arrested and forced to train as a slave gladiator. In 73 BC he led a break-out of around seventy gladiators from the gladiator school at Capua. They hid on Mount Vesuvius and when besieged on the mountain they escaped down ladders made of wild vines. Soon other escaped slaves flocked to join them. By the following year Spartacus commanded an army of 90,000 men.

Spartacus defeated several Roman armies, but his men had no discipline. They started to behave like criminals, murdering, looting and attacking whenever they could. He realized that such a rabble was no longer able to fight properly and pleaded with them to escape with him from Italy. His men refused - they were having too much of a good time!

When Roman billionaire Crassus led yet another army against them in 71 BC, the escaped slaves fought bravely but were defeated. Spartacus was killed and six thousand of his men were crucified 🦶 *along the main road to Rome from the south.*

🦶 Crucifixion was a painful form of punishment reserved for slaves and the worst criminals. The victim was either nailed or tied to a wooden cross and left to die. It was an unusual method of execution for a free man such as Jesus Christ, who was crucified in AD 33.

SLAVE YOURSELF THE BOTHER

Slaves were so cheap at the height of the Empire that rich people owned hundreds or even thousands of them. Some owners couldn't do anything for themselves:

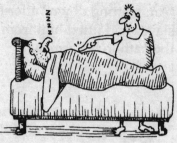

Slaves reminded them to go to bed at night and woke them in the morning.

'Human clock' slaves called out the time.

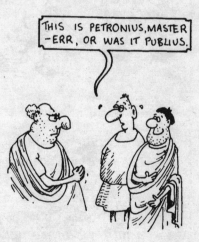

Some slaves did nothing but stand around and look good.

Nomenclatores remembered the names of visitors.

Slaves did everything for their owners. They bathed them, combed their hair and got them dressed. The writer Seneca describes one man as asking: 'Am I sitting down?' after his slaves had lifted him from the bath to his armchair.

Another man was so unused to walking that he had a slave walk before him when he did, to point out any bumps in the road and to remind his master not to walk into things. There were even slaves to do their owners' thinking: one man had a slave to stand behind his chair at dinner parties and tell him clever things to say.

It was fashionable for dinner guests to dry their hands in slaves' hair.

Household slaves might be pampered like favourite pets, but others were not so lucky. Some Roman farms in Britain have been found with special underground prisons with chains where the farm workers were kept at night. One rich Roman woman reckoned it was cheaper to work her slaves to death and then to get new ones than to feed them properly.

It wasn't all bad. Every December at Saturnalia, the festival of the god Saturn, the tables were turned and slaves were waited on by their masters. Christians replaced Saturnalia with a new winter festival - Christmas.

TO FREE OR NOT TO FREE

Slavery is one of the hardest things for us to understand about the Romans. How could they believe that a slave was just a 'tame animal', and also that the same slave became a human being immediately he or she was freed? And if slaves *were* no better than animals, how come so many were freed? After all you're unlikely to free a real animal such as a cow. The writer Cicero reckoned that on average a slave would be freed after only six years of slavery, though he may have been exaggerating.

The lowest age at which a slave was allowed to be free was thirty. Many were freed as soon as they reached that age. Others might save up their *peculium* and buy themselves from their owners. Many more were freed at the death of their owners, and a lucky handful even inherited their owners' property. There were so many ex-slaves and the children of ex-slaves that it's reckoned that everyone in Rome had at least one slave ancestor, even the aristocrats.

YOU SAY YOU'RE DESCENDED FROM FELIX SLAVONICUS — FUNNY SORT OF NAME, ISN'T IT?

IT'S THE LAW, CITIZENS!

The first Roman laws were very tough. They gave a lot of authority to the male head of the family, known as the *paterfamilias*. Fathers could and sometimes did execute their children if they committed certain crimes. However things softened as the years went by, until by the end there were even laws to protect slaves, and slaves could no longer be killed by their owners without 'good' reason.

THIS IS FOR YOUR OWN GOOD, CORNELIUS.

The *peculium* was money a slave managed to save for him or herself from tips and other small payments.

The first Roman laws were made in 753 BC and the last in the west in AD 535. Being Roman laws, they were all efficiently written down. There was no shortage; by the end there were three million judgements written out in twenty-six volumes! Roman law is still the basis for most law in Europe.

IF A SLAVE KILLS HIMSELF, IS THIS AN ACT OF THEFT? LET'S LOOK AT THE CASE OF PAULUS POSTUMUS AND THE MAD SLAVE.

At first, the only people having full rights and duties under the law were the *paterfamilias* or heads of families. These were the first Roman citizens. Only citizens could use Roman law courts or appeal to the Emperor in Rome. Even as the Empire expanded, everyone else had to make do with local laws, which were different in different places. But ex-legionnaires became citizens automatically on retirement, and gradually, by this and other means, citizenship was given to most of the people of Italy and to some in places beyond. Saint Paul, one of the founders of Christianity, was a Roman citizen even though he was Jewish. Finally in AD 212 Emperor Caracalla gave citizenship to almost all the free inhabitants of the Empire, including the Romano-Britons.

The Ancient Britons had been changed from spiky-haired, blue-painted savages into citizens of the most powerful Empire on Earth in just 150 years from the time of their defeat by Claudius' army.

Or so it seemed ...

He was born in Gaul and used to wear a hooded tunic called a *caracalla*, which is why he's always called Caracalla. His real name was *Marcus Aurelius Antoninus*.

NITTY GRITTY CITIES

FANCY FORUMS AND BUSY BASILICAS

THE THREE Cs

Cities go with civilization like tomatoes go with ketchup. In fact, our words *citizen*, *city* and *civilization* all come from the Latin word for a city: *civitas*. Before the Romans there were no cities in Britain - and no civilization in the way of books, laws, paintings, home comforts and things like that. The best the Ancient Britons could manage was the odd scruffy collection of huts around the big hut of the local king or queen.

The Romans lost no time in changing all that. Towns sprang up like dandelions on a cabbage patch. You can hardly move in England without bumping into towns started by the Romans.

> If the name of your town ends in 'eter' 'cester' or 'chester', 'caistor' 'caister' 'cetter' or 'caster', like Exeter, Gloucester and Chester, you can be sure that it was started by the Romans. All these word endings come originally from the Latin word *castor*, meaning a military camp.

A Roman's home is Rome

It's no wonder the Romans built cities. After all, Rome was a city before it became the head of an Empire as well. And it was the largest city in the world. Rome had the greatest temples, the greatest theatres, the greatest circuses and amphitheatres  . Water was brought from far outside the town on the greatest aqueducts. Cities throughout the Empire copied it.

It's reckoned that at the time of the great fire of AD 64 *two million* people lived there. That meant two million Romans to be fed, watered and kept happy without any of the modern technology we take for granted, such as computers, cars and television. Despite the lack of technology, in many ways it was quite like a modern city. It even had traffic jams: heavy

Circuses and ampitheatres were a bit like football stadiums today. They were where people went to watch horse races and other more gruesome games. More on that later.

The citizens blamed Nero for the fire. He is said to have played his lyre as the flames roared through the city. Nero in turn blamed the early Christians for starting it.

goods wagons were only allowed into the city at night so as to reduce traffic. People complained that the noise of wooden wheels on the streets paved with dark grey rock was deafening.

OLD SOLDIERS' HOMES

The first cities in Britain were built by soldiers who had retired from the Roman army. When they started their three *colonies*  at Colchester, Gloucester and Lincoln they made sure the temples and other public buildings were in the Roman style, to make a real home from home. The houses were often built within old army camps as at Colchester, so being old soldiers no doubt they felt doubly at home.

See page 35, *colonies* were settlements of retired Roman soldiers.

'Lincoln' is short for *Lindum Colonium*, meaning a *colony* in *Lindum* (roughly modern Lincolnshire).

Emperors liked colonies because the old soldiers showed the natives how to live a civilized life the Roman way, and Emperors wanted everyone to become Roman or to 'wear the toga'  as Julius Caesar put it. Once in their new homes, the old codgers settled down to farm - on land that had recently belonged to the defeated Britons.

New towns were built by the recently-defeated Britons as well. They took longer to get started than the Romans because they didn't have experience of building, except for huts and hill-forts. The Romans helped out by lending military engineers, so the new British-built towns also looked a bit like army barracks. The first two were Canterbury and St Albans.

Later, London (known as *Augustus* for a long time) grew to be the largest town and the city of Bath, known to the Romans as *Aquae Sulis*, was the poshest because Romano-Britons went there to relax in the natural hot springs. You can still see the remains of the Roman baths at Bath.

The *toga* was the standard Roman garment. More about that later.

CONSENTIUS'S CLASSICAL CONTOURS

Consentius the classical architect has designed a classical 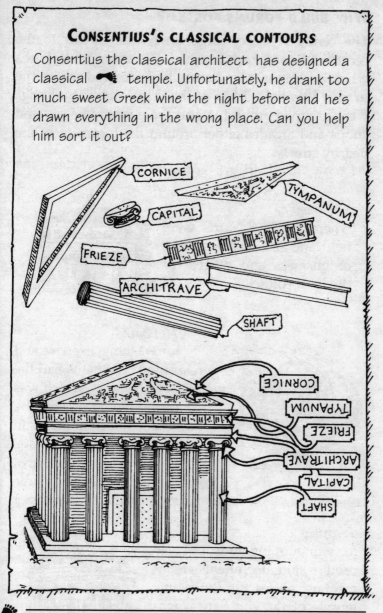 temple. Unfortunately, he drank too much sweet Greek wine the night before and he's drawn everything in the wrong place. Can you help him sort it out?

CORNICE

TYMPANUM

CAPITAL

FRIEZE

ARCHITRAVE

SHAFT

CORNICE

TYPANUM

FRIEZE

ARCHITRAVE

CAPITAL

SHAFT

The word *classical* means, among other things, 'of Ancient Greek or Roman culture'.

WHY BUILD FORUMS FOR'EM?

The centre of every large town was similar to the centre of Rome. Each one had a *forum*, a central area where people met to discuss business and where the market was held. Most of the major public buildings were grouped around it, and there would be covered shops and arcades either around the forum or in the nearby streets.

PUBLIC PLACES

The basilica
where the law courts were held, and also used as a place of business and offices for the local council.

The baths
for washing, exercise and relaxation. The baths had the main public lavatory, which was flushed into the sewer by outflow water from the main pools. There was no toilet paper. Toilet-users shared a piece of cloth or a sponge tied on a pole and kept in a tub of salty water.

Temples
for worshipping gods, but also used to store documents and as meeting places. In Rome, the temple of the god Saturn was the State Treasury.

Amphitheatre
where shows were put on.

MAJESTIC MOMENT

COULD *YOU* BE A ROMAN? (PART 3)

Consentius the architect has drunk too much wine again. He's been causing a nuisance and has to go to court. You are the magistrate. Where would you find your court room? (Answer on page 122)

a In the temple of Saturn
b Above a wine shop at the back of the forum
c In the basilica

HOME TRUTHS

The rich often had a large town house, or *domus*, as well as a villa in the country. The *domus* of a patrician was normally a large inward looking building, perhaps with shops set in the outside walls. There were plenty of rooms, and husband and wife had

67

separate bedrooms (slaves were usually crammed into small rooms in the cellar). The houses of the rich had their own central heating and indoor toilet. In fact, an indoor toilet was something to boast about as an expensive car might be today.

Things were different for the poor. In Rome and in many other towns the majority of the population lived in blocks of flats called *insulae*. The cheapest flats were at the top where, in Rome at least, cooking was forbidden for fear of fires. There were no toilets. If you needed the toilet, you had to find a public toilet - or throw muck into the street.

 'Cave' means 'beware'.

DRUSILLA'S VILLA

LIFE IN THE COUNTRY

Drusilla has just got married. She's about to move into her husband's new *villa*.

HUT OR VILLA?

Cities may have been necessary for civilization, but most British people lived on small farms and spoke Celtic for the whole time that the Romans ruled Britain.

But gradually rich farmers started to build *villas*, which is Latin for 'country houses'. Villas were as different from Celtic huts as the Tower of London is from a bouncy castle. They were solidly built with plenty of rooms and they had all the Roman comforts such as central heating.

THAT HUT IS AN EYESORE, PETRONIUS

HERE IT IS - DRUSILLA'S VILLA

Drusilla's fiancé is a rich Romano-Briton called Didius. He's just built this amazing new villa for them to live in together.

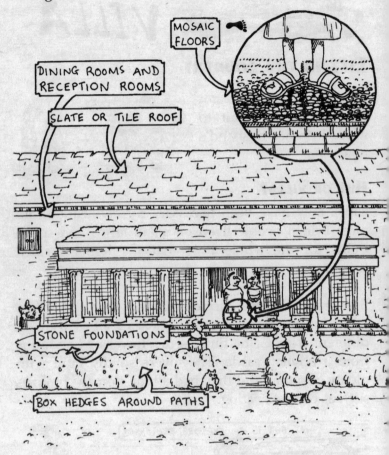

MOSAIC FLOORS

DINING ROOMS AND RECEPTION ROOMS

SLATE OR TILE ROOF

STONE FOUNDATIONS

BOX HEDGES AROUND PATHS

The main crops grown on British villa estates would have been barley, wheat and beans, but villa owners

Mosaics are pictures or patterns made up of lots of small pieces of different coloured stone.

aimed to be self-sufficient in almost everything. They even grew their own wine - when they were allowed to.

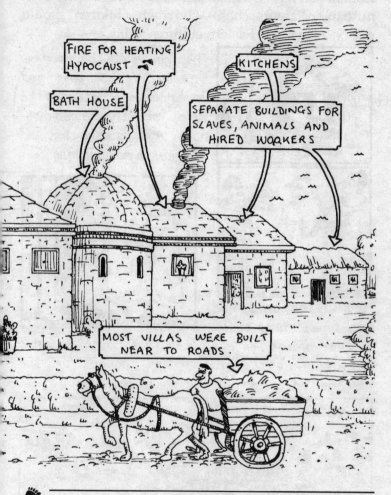

FIRE FOR HEATING HYPOCAUST

KITCHENS

BATH HOUSE

SEPARATE BUILDINGS FOR SLAVES, ANIMALS AND HIRED WORKERS

MOST VILLAS WERE BUILT NEAR TO ROADS.

In the first century AD so much land throughout the Empire was given over to producing wine instead of wheat that the Emperor Domitian forbade all wine-growing outside Italy. It was only in the third century that the British were allowed to grow wine again.

A *hypocaust* was a central heating system. Normally hot air was circulated under the floor.

71

Drusilla's marriage

Drusilla and Didius have decided to get married in Roman style. Drusilla did not choose her own husband. Parents chose who their children should marry, as in some Eastern cultures today.

The night before the marriage Drusilla left her toys and young maiden's clothes in the care of the household gods to show that she was now an adult woman.

Next day she wore a white wool tunic, orange shoes, a short orange veil and put a wreath of the herb marjoram on her head.

Then the bridegroom came to her house for the ceremony and a feast.

Later the happy couple walked in a procession to their new house, chanting marriage hymns to the gods.

 Called *lares*. More on these later.

Once they got to the villa, Drusilla rubbed oil and fat on the doorposts and wound wool round them in a traditional Roman ceremony. Then Didius carried her over the threshold.

Kids' stuff

Once they were married, a young couple would expect to have children, but sadly not many of those children would grow up to become adults. The British gravestone of one centurion's wife, aged only twenty-seven at the time of her death, shows that she had already had seven children and that only one was still alive.

But never mind: surplus children were killed off anyway. The Romans were ruthless - malformed or unwanted children were exposed to die on the hillsides outside Rome from earliest times. The remains of nearly one hundred new-born babies have been found beside a villa at Hambleden in Buckinghamshire.

HAAAAH!

BAAH? BAA

The children of the poor and of slaves would have had to start work at an early age. But the kids of the rich didn't work and had a wide range of toys to play with. Here are a few of them:

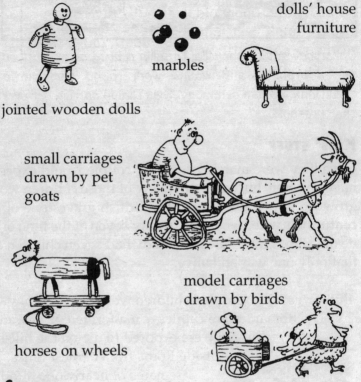

jointed wooden dolls

marbles

dolls' house furniture

small carriages drawn by pet goats

horses on wheels

model carriages drawn by birds

School

Both boys and girls went to primary school from the ages of six or seven. The school was often a room close to the forum of the local town. The pupils were taken there by their *pedagogues*, slaves who looked after them and heard them recite their lessons. In the case of Drusilla's children this might have meant a journey of several kilometres there and back each day between the villa and the town.

The main lessons were reading and writing, which was practised either by scratching letters on a wax-coated wooden board or by writing with ink and a reed pen. It was Roman schools that finally killed off the power of the Druids, because the poor old Druids didn't believe in reading and writing. This put them at a big disadvantage when it came to winning young followers.

READING AGAIN, CATARACT? HAND ME THE BOOK, YOU DISMAL BOY!

A DRUID

Later, the boys went on to a *grammaticus* where they studied difficult subjects such as Greek, poetry and grammar under a well-educated teacher. Because most Romano-Britons spoke Celtic at home, Drusilla's boys could have ended up speaking three languages - Greek, Latin and Celtic.

Teachers at the grammaticus had to know their subjects. Because teaching wasn't very well paid, to encourage people to do the job the wages were tax-free. Discipline was harsh and teachers knew how to keep order: several carvings of teachers holding sticks have been found.

Then at fifteen the brightest boys went on to a *rhetor*, a teacher who taught them how to speak in public. This was an important skill in Roman times.

While the bright boys went to the rhetor, at fifteen the girls were ready to get married. Which is where we started this chapter with Drusilla.

THE GOOD LIFE

LIVING IT UP AT BANQUETS, AND OTHER BASHES

Rich Celts took to the Roman way of life like ducks to water. Who can blame them? With slaves to tend to your every whim, there was plenty of time for the luxuries of life, such as getting ready for dinner.

WE DINE AT NINE

Drusilla and Didius have been invited to dinner in a nearby villa. Dinner started at around four in the afternoon, or the 'ninth hour' as the Romans would have called it, because they didn't number the hours in the same way that we do.

DIDIUS DARLING, THE DINNRI HAVE INVITED US TO DINNER. I'LL BE DARNED IF I'VE GOT ANYTHING DECENT TO WEAR.

FIVE PAST FIVE, SIX PAST FIVE, SEVEN...

A GOOD SCRAPE

Every villa had its own bath house, or several of them. They were smaller versions of the big public baths in the towns. A large villa like Drusilla's would have a room for getting undressed, a room for a cold plunge, a *tepidarium* or warm room and a steam room like a sauna. The Celts used a sort of soap, but if a rich Briton chose to follow the Roman fashion, he or she would be covered in olive oil then scraped clean by a slave using a curved metal instrument called a *strigil*.

GOOD-LOOKING OR WHAT?

It's unlikely the *dominus*, or owner, of a British villa would have paid as much attention to himself as a smooth dresser in Rome. After all, who was he going to meet on a daily basis apart from his wife and children, his slaves and the odd cow? Besides, his poorer neighbours might still be painting themselves with woad and laugh at him.

But if he was going out to dinner the dominus would probably make an effort. After all, the ancient Greeks and Romans thought that beauty was a virtue, in fact one of the highest virtues ☜. Back in Rome, some men spent a lot of time and money on looking good ...

It was the custom of the Ancient Britons to paint or tattoo themselves with blue dye from the woad plant.

The Emperor Septimus Severus ate hare every day because it was meant to help you stay good looking.

79

They might paint their faces, including highlights on their skin. If they were going bald, they might wear false hair to cover the bald patch or even paint pretend hair over it! The Emperor Gallienus powdered his hair with gold dust. It's hard to imagine a Romano-British villa-owner going quite so far.

THE MILKY WAY

It wouldn't do to disturb a rich Roman woman while she was sleeping: you might get an unpleasant shock. She might be wearing a *poppaeana*, a face mask invented by Nero's wife Poppaea. The poppaeana was a mixture of dough and asses' milk worn on the face at night to improve the complexion. There was another

type of face mask made of rice and beanflour which was meant to remove wrinkles. Face masks were washed off in the morning with a rinse of luke-warm asses' milk.

In fact asses' milk seems to have been the ultimate beauty aid. Cleopatra bathed in it every day. Some women washed their faces in it several times a day. Poppaea never travelled anywhere without a herd of female asses so she wouldn't run out.

After the asses' milk treatment, most women painted their faces with red and white paint moistened with spit. Veins on the forehead might be highlighted with blue. Eyebrows and eyelashes were either dyed black or painted.

TUNICS AND TOGAS

Having bathed, done your hair and put on some make-up, the only thing left before leaving for dinner would be to get dressed, which in Roman times meant the two Ts - tunics or togas. Togas soon became fashionable among upper class Celts.

Togas were pieces of cloth about three times as long as the height of an average man and very difficult to wear. They were worn on smart formal occasions. At fifteen a boy would climb into a pure white *toga virilis*, the symbol of adulthood, and leave his youthful purple-fringed *toga praetextas* on the bedroom floor. Women also wore togas or a similar garment over their tunics, or *stolas*. At around fifteen girls also stepped out of their youthful purple-edged togas and were ready for marriage.

WAYS TO WEAR A TOGA
Part 1. (the only part there is)

WRONG

RIGHT

Tunics were comfortable everyday clothes, normally made of two pieces of cloth sewn up the sides and cut the same for both men and women.

OTHER THINGS TO DO WITH A TOGA

TAKE YOUR PLACE

Six was thought to be the ideal number for a small dinner party, although there was always space for nine, and obviously large banquets seated - or rather 'lay' - many more.

Romans ate lying down, which must have been very uncomfortable until you got used to it. The left arm took your weight and the right hand was for eating. Mainly they used knives, spoons and fingers. There were no forks. To make things a little easier, the low couches which they lay on were tilted slightly towards the table. Each couch had space for three people lying at an angle.

Dining-rooms were usually furnished with three couches arranged in a 'U' shape with a table in the middle. Slaves used the empty space in the middle for serving food.

TIME TO DINE

Poor people ate a simple diet of bread and other basic foods. But if possible nearly everyone spiced their food with *liquamen* which was the ketchup of the ancient world. Liquamen was basically rotten-fish-juice. It was salty, fishy, pale yellow and cheesy and Romans loved it.

RECIPE FOR LIQUAMEN

There were many different kinds of liquamen.
Here's the recipe of the famous Roman gourmet
Apicius:

2. Leave
overnight.

1. Mix up some fish in a 'baking
trough' with a lot of salt.

3. Cram into an earthenware
container and leave open in the sun
for up to three months, stirring
from time to time.

4. Cover and store
away. You can add
some old wine at
this stage.

5. Strain out the pale yellow
residue and leave to mature.

MAD MORSELS

In Rome a normal meal might include fish, leeks,
chick-peas, lupins and sausages, which are still cooked
in roughly the same way in Italy today, two thousand
years later. Nothing very exotic, apart from the lupins.
The food in Britain would have been a bit different
because of the northern climate. British oysters and
mussels were very popular.

CAN'T EAT IT!

For a swanky banquet things became very elaborate. Details of many meals were written down. Which of these tasty trifles were not eaten by Romans? (**Answers upside down**):

potatoes

parrots' heads

tomatoes

camels' heels

ostrich heads

elephants' trunks

pearls

nightingales's brains

dormice sprinkled with honey and poppy seeds

What the Romans called *dormouse* was actually our field mouse. They were specially bred in hutches.

IT'S ENOUGH TO MAKE YOU SICK

Romans could eat a lot of food. The Emperor Vitellius once gave a banquet where two thousand costly fish and seven thousand birds were dished up. It was hard to eat so much food and some people had to make use of *vomitoria*, in other words they made themselves sick, often by tickling the back of the throat with a feather.

Many did this for health reasons since regular vomitings had been recommended by doctors since the time of the ancient Greek doctor, Hippocrates. But a lot of them did it just so they could eat some more. They 'vomited to eat, and ate to vomit,' as the writer Seneca put it.

GLADIATORS!

LEISURE TIME THE ROMAN WAY

You can't eat dinner all day. With so much leisure time on our hands we Romans demanded other amusements.

ARE YOU GAME FOR A GAME?

Romano-Britons liked to play, but 'games' were different then from how they are now. If a friend asks you to 'watch the game' with him or her, you probably assume that means a game of football. In Roman times it would probably have meant the spectacle of gladiators hacking each other to death.

ERE WE GO, 'ERE WE GO, 'ERE WE GO, HERE WE GO, 'ERE WE GO-OH....

Roman games were put on either by the local council or by a rich citizen to show off his wealth. Entry was free, so staging games was a good way for a rich local politician to please the common people.

COLOSSAL OR WHAT? - THE COLOSSEUM

Games were staged in circuses and amphitheatres. Five amphitheatres have been found in Britain . The rows for the seats were dug out of curving hill sides so that they looked down on the central stage area. They were used for all kinds of popular entertainment as well as 'games'.

1000 SAILORS WERE NEEDED TO WINCH OUT THE CANOPY (VELARIUM), USING 160 WINCHES

50,000 WAGON LOADS OF LIMESTONE WERE USED IN THE CONSTRUCTION, BROUGHT ALONG A SPECIALLY MADE ROAD FROM THE QUARRY

5 TONNE BLOCKS OF STONE AT THE BASE OF THE PILLARS

At Dorchester, Silchester, Chichester, Cirencester and Carmarthen.

Compared to what was on offer in Rome, British amphitheatres were puny, pathetic and provincial. Rome had the *Colosseum*, which was absolutely massive. And in Rome the Emperor organized the games: he didn't want other wealthy men to get too popular.

CAPACITY FOR 45-50,000 SPECTATORS

DARK CELLS BELOW GROUND FOR PRISONERS, ANIMALS AND GLADIATORS

TAME GAMES – AND NOT SO TAME

Early Roman games were based on Ancient Greek athletic competitions and included events such as the pentathlon. But athletics were too tame for Romans, who looked down on them. The famous doctor Galen said they made men 'idle, sleepy and slow-witted'.

Romans preferred the sports of their near neighbours, the Etruscans . Etruscan warriors used to fight to the death outside the tombs of dead chiefs as a form of sacrifice. For four hundred years Roman gladiator fights were also only staged at funerals. But gradually things started to change ...

THIS IS MORE LIKE IT!

GLAD. TO BE BAD

Gladiatorial fights became more and more popular. By the time the Colosseum opened in AD 80 they had become the main attraction in the games. In fact two

The *Etruscans* ruled northern Italy before the Romans came along, and much of Roman civilization was copied from the Etruscans. In fact the three kings of Rome before it became a republic were Etruscan. No one has been able to decipher their writing. We know very little about them.

thousand people were killed in the Colosseum's arena within the first two weeks of the grand opening. Soon a constant supply of fresh fighters was needed to replace those who died.

There was never any shortage: gladiators were mostly either convicts, slaves or prisoners of war who had no choice but to fight. Few of them lived to old age; only a handful of fighters who won lots of fights were given the wooden sword of retirement and could live on as instructors.

The sport was so popular that some noblemen took it up (although it was always looked down on as an inferior occupation). There were even Emperors who played at being gladiators, which tended to be an unpleasant experience for the people they were fighting ...

Caligula fought an opponent who was armed with only a wooden sword - Caligula had a real one. Guess who won!

When the Emperor Commodus was in the ring with his bow and arrow, the people in the front rows were always nervous in case he decided to pick off a few spectators.

To provide variety for the audience, there were also women gladiators. Nero loved to watch them. They were eventually banned by the Emperor Septimus Severus in AD 200.

BAK TO SKOOL

Gladiators trained in special gladiator schools such as the one Spartacus escaped from at Capua. The gladiator school at Pompeii had seventy-one small sleeping rooms arranged in two stories around a practice hall. They practised with wooden swords and blunt weapons.

There were several types of gladiator:

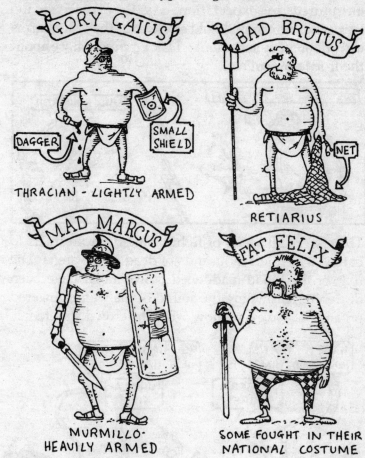

GORY GAIUS

DAGGER

SMALL SHIELD

THRACIAN - LIGHTLY ARMED

BAD BRUTUS

NET

RETIARIUS

MAD MARCUS

MURMILLO-
HEAVILY ARMED

FAT FELIX

SOME FOUGHT IN THEIR
NATIONAL COSTUME

GET ON WITH IT!

The evening before a fight the gladiators were given a special feast. Their loved ones came to say goodbye and the curious came to gawp at them while they ate. It was a sad occasion.

Next day they marched round the arena on the gleaming sand soon to be drenched in the blood of the slain, while around them the fifty thousand spectators murmured in expectation. As they reached the Emperor's box they would stretch out their right arms in front of them and shout : 'Hail Emperor, those about to die salute you!'.

There were all kinds of fights, ranging from duels to battles which left thousands of dead in the arena. The roar of the blood-maddened crowd must have been deafening, drowning the sound of the water-powered organ 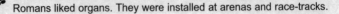. We even know what the crowd shouted:

Romans liked organs. They were installed at arenas and race-tracks.

Hoc habet!

If defeated, a gladiator threw away his shield and raised a finger of his left hand as an appeal for mercy. The winner then decided whether or not to kill him, unless the Emperor was present, in which case the Emperor decided. The crowd helped with advice. Either they waved their handkerchiefs and put their thumbs up shouting: '*Mitte!*', meaning 'let him go', or they put their thumbs down and shouted: '*Iugula!*' meaning 'kill'. If the Emperor turned his thumb down the loser was killed immediately.

One slight reminder of ancient Etruscan customs remained. A man dressed as Charon , the Etruscan minister of fate, poked the dead with hot irons or struck him on the forehead with a hammer to make sure he was not faking . Finally slaves rushed on to the arena to shovel up the blood-soaked sand and sprinkle fresh sand before the next fight.

The Ancient Greeks also believed in a figure called Charon, but he was different. The Greek Charon was an old man who ferried dead souls to the Greek paradise of Elysium.

Animal magic

The Romans loved animals - as entertainment. Some Emperors kept apes trained to drive chariots and sea-lions were taught to bark in answer to their names. There was even a group of four elephants trained to sit down to dinner and to carry a fifth in a litter.

WHO NEEDS STRAWS?

But what Romans liked best of all was watching animals being killed - or killing. It was almost better sport than the gladiators. The animals were shot and speared by specialists called *bestiarii*. Nine thousand animals were killed in the arena in the first hundred days after the Colosseum was opened.

Sometimes the animals were given a chance, as when naked spearman were matched against lions or leopards. At other times it was straightforward butchery, as when well-armed men speared harmless animals such as giraffes. And sometimes the animals had the advantage, as when unarmed Christians were pitted against lions by the Emperor Nero.

THE ANTICS OF ANDROCLES

Androcles was a Christian slave. He escaped from slavery and while he was on the run he hid in a cave. Unfortunately, or so it seemed, a lion entered the cave after him. But instead of gobbling him up, the lion held out its paw. Androcles saw that it was suffering from a large thorn embedded in its pad. He removed the thorn. The lion did not hurt him.

Later Androcles was recaptured and sentenced to fight a lion in the arena. Amazingly the lion which bounded towards him turned out to be the very same lion that he had helped previously.

Instead of attacking him the lion became all friendly and Androcles and the lion were allowed to live. Tradition has it that after the games were over, Androcles took his lion from inn to inn on a rope, collecting money.

There was no limit to the slaughter of animals. From the farthest corners of the known world, wagon loads of captive creatures were trundled off to the Colosseum and the other amphitheatres of the Empire. No doubt a fair number found their way to Britain. Agents searched for rare and exotic creatures. In many regions, whole species were hunted out of existence. By the end of the Empire, there were no more lions in Mesopotamia, no more elephants in North Africa, no more tigers by the Caspian Sea.

CHARIOT FEVER

Gladiators were great, but the ultimate Roman sporting passion was chariot racing. It was almost a disease among them. There were four teams: Red, White, Blue and Green. People were fanatical about their teams, just as some people are fanatical about football teams today. One supporter of the Reds threw himself on the funeral pyre of his favourite jockey! Everyone from highest to lowest was involved. Nero had green sand sprinkled on the race track - guess which team he supported!

Fanatics would even sniff the dung of the horses to check that they were being well fed.

HMM, OATS WITH A PINCH OF BARLEY.

Modern football hooligans are bunny-rabbits compared to Roman chariot hooligans. In the Nika Riot of AD 532 in Constantinople between supporters of the Greens and the Blues, *30,000 people* are said to have died!

BLUES! GREENS!

COME TO THE CIRCUS

Chariot races were held in long oval race tracks called circuses. No remains of circuses have been found in Britain as yet, but it's hard to believe that the Romano-Britons didn't like chariot racing, given that the Celts had been such expert charioteers before the Romans came.

HUGE EGGS AND DOLPHINS WERE TAKEN DOWN ONE BY ONE TO COUNT THE NUMBER OF CIRCUITS.

GLISTENING SAND

Circus Maximus means 'Biggest Circus', and that's exactly what the Circus Maximus in Rome was - the biggest circus in the world. It could seat 150,000 spectators, some sitting on comfy cushions which they could buy at the entrance.

THE CENTRE WAS USED TO SHOW OFF PRISONERS OF WAR AND OTHER LOOT.

FAMOUS CHARIOTEERS WERE STARS.

EITHER TWO OR FOUR HORSES - USUALLY

REINS TIED AROUND WAIST

SLAVES ON DUTY AT THE CORNERS THREW BUCKETS OF WATER ON THE AXLES TO COOL THEM.

KNIFE TO CUT REINS IN AN ACCIDENT

NOTHING LASTS FOR EVER

We don't race chariots any more, and it's impossible to find a proper gladiator fight nowadays. All things come to an end.

In AD 402 a Christian monk called Telemachus tried to throw himself between two gladiators to stop them fighting. The official presiding over the games had him killed immediately. But when word of this reached the ear of the Emperor Honorius, he banned the games and they were never played again.

Chariot racing continued for a while longer. The last chariot race in Rome was run in an empty, ruined city in AD 549 in the presence of the barbarian invader, Totila the Goth.

ODD GODS

GLORIOUS GODS AND CRITICAL CHRISTIANS

SIX SPECIAL GODS

There were at least thirty thousand Roman gods. They ranged from the small and unusual 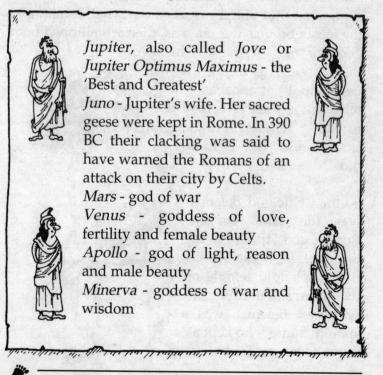 to the grand and magnificent, such as Jove the greatest of all. Here are a few of the most important:

Jupiter, also called *Jove* or *Jupiter Optimus Maximus* - the 'Best and Greatest'

Juno - Jupiter's wife. Her sacred geese were kept in Rome. In 390 BC their clacking was said to have warned the Romans of an attack on their city by Celts.

Mars - god of war

Venus - goddess of love, fertility and female beauty

Apollo - god of light, reason and male beauty

Minerva - goddess of war and wisdom

As an example of an unusual sort of god, how about *Robigus* the god of red mildew?

What's the difference?

Roman religion was very matter-of-fact. You said your prayers and made your sacrifices and then you got on with life. To be a priest was a mark of honour and good for your career. People were often given priesthoods in the way they are given knighthoods today.

Romans believed that everyone in the world worshipped the same basic gods, it's just that they called them by different names. This was a very convenient idea. Whatever country the Romans conquered they simply worked out what Roman god the local god was the same as, then worshipped both gods or one of them, whichever they chose. This meant that they never took offence at foreign religions, unless of course the foreign religion caused trouble like the Druids' did.

So the Celtic god *Belenus* was the same as the Roman god *Apollo*. It was just that in Rome Apollo had a splendid temple on the forum and in Britain he, or rather Belenus, was a spooky figure who kept a raven as his pet bird.

Similarly the mischievous, goat-horned, goat-legged

minor god *Pan* was the same as the horned Celtic god *Cernunnos*. And the Roman goddess of war and wisdom *Minerva* was the same as the Celtic goddess *Sul*. In fact the city of *Aquae Sulis* (modern Bath) was often called *Aquae Sulis Minerva*.

A PACKET OF GODLETS

They also believed in a whole host of little gods. The little gods and demons would carry messages to the top gods if you asked them nicely , perhaps with a little sacrifice. There was a whole host of demigods such as *centaurs* who were half man and half horse, and *satyrs* who had legs like goats. In every house there was a *lararium*, normally a cupboard in the form of a miniature temple. This was where the household gods, the *lares* and *penates* were kept.

Everything had its *genius,* or guardian spirit. There was a genius for every place and for every different group of people: every legion had its own genius.

Means 'Waters of Sul'.

Pre-Christian Romans could never understand why Christians thought Christianity was so different to other religions. After all, Christians believed in angels, which behaved pretty much like Roman demons.

That's why the Romans could come up with the mad idea of making their Emperors into gods: in a sense the Emperor, or at least his reign, already had a genius or spirit. So why not worship it?

OH GOD!

Kings and emperors had been worshipped as gods in many civilizations before the time of the Romans, but it was Julius Caesar who started the fashion in Rome. He claimed 'divine honours' before he died. The first actual Roman emperor to be worshipped as a god was Augustus (63 BC - AD 14), although his godliness wasn't made official until after his death.

Soon the *Imperial Cult* as it was known became an important part of Roman rule. It was a good way of binding together all the different nations which made up the Empire. That's why almost as soon as they had conquered Britain the Romans built a massive temple to the Emperor Claudius at Colchester.

EASTERN MYSTERIES

Towards the end of the Empire several religions or cults from countries to the east became popular. The three most important were *Mithraism* from Persia, the worship of the Ancient Egyptian goddess *Isis*, and

Christianity which started in Palestine among followers of the Jewish religion.

MITHRAS

Temples dedicated to Mithras have been found all over the Empire including in London and on Hadrian's Wall. He was a spirit of pure light, and high moral standards were expected of his followers. They behaved a bit like Christians, holding sacred meals similar to Holy Communion as well as other secret rituals, although some of their rituals were rather different to the Christians' - for instance, having to lie under an iron grill while a bull was slaughtered on top of you.

ISIS

Isis was incredibly ancient, being one of the first Egyptian gods. She was a goddess of protection and healing. Her followers worshipped her in noisy ceremonies. She was very popular.

CHRIST

Christ was a Jew who had been crucified by the Romans. His followers believed in love and that Christ would return to Earth within a few years to save them and take them to heaven.

MAD MARTYRS

The Romans took a violent dislike to the Christians. The main problem was that, like the Jews, the Christians refused to recognize other people's gods.

Just imagine: you're a pagan, you've sown your fields

with coins so as to buy a good harvest from Ceres, the goddess of corn . Your neighbour is a Christian who not only doesn't sow his fields with coins, but goes out of his way to say that Ceres doesn't exist, thereby annoying Ceres, who then gets mad and stops the rain. It's enough to turn anyone off Christianity.

Romans devised a test to smoke out the Christians. Everyone was ordered to worship the Emperor. They had to pour some sacred oil then make a sacrifice and eat the meat. Anyone who refused could be executed. Many Christians refused, even when kind-hearted Roman officials pleaded with them, and offered to allow them to burn a little incense instead of making a sacrifice.

In several great waves of executions, Christians were fed to lions, burnt alive, crucified and disposed of in a hundred cruel ways. Their torture was the main attraction at many games.

To make matters worse, the Christians often welcomed their persecution. There were even volunteers! They firmly believed that whoever died for the faith, becoming a *martyr*, would go to heaven. They were so sure of this that very unchristian orgies took place in the cells beneath some North African arenas, among Christians waiting to be killed (after all they were going to go to heaven anyway): so much so that the local bishops had to write letters telling them to stop it.

This custom is why so many Roman coins are still found in our fields.

110

CONSTANTINE - A VERY IMPORTANT PERSON

Constantine's mother was the daughter of an innkeeper, but his father Constantius was a Caesar (a lesser position than emperor at that time). He took after his father and as soon as he was adult, he went after power like a bull terrier after a bone.

In AD 306 Constantius died at York after fighting in Scotland, beyond Hadrian's Wall. So it was at York that Constantine, who was one of his father's commanders, was declared Emperor by his father's army. He went on to defeat all his rivals and became a very powerful Roman Emperor. The reason he's so important is that he was the first Christian Emperor 🐾 . It happened before his last great battle which was with a rival Emperor called Maxentius. Constantine saw a vision of a flaming cross in the sky. Because of this vision he believed that Christ helped him win the battle.

Constantine wasn't a Christian as most people might understand the word today; he murdered his wife and his son. But in AD 342 he made Christianity the state religion of the Empire - and changed the world.

Constantine is also famous for making ancient Byzantium, which he called *Constantinople* (modern Istanbul), the capital of the Eastern Roman Empire.

Do as you have been done by

After AD 342 Christianity swept through the Empire like a bush fire. Christians started popping up everywhere. After all, you now had to be a Christian to get a good job working for the Empire. The Christians lost no time in getting rid of the old Roman gods. It was Christians who destroyed the shrines and statues of the old religion.

Within a hundred years you could hardly find a follower of the old gods anywhere except in the deepest countryside. That's why followers of the old religion became known as *pagans*, from *paganus,* the Latin word for a country yokel or villager.

Nowadays pagan tends to mean an irreligious person - but perhaps Jupiter wouldn't have minded.

BEASTLY BARBARIANS

THE BEGINNING OF THE END

Like a cat with fleas, the Roman Empire was always scratching itself. Except they weren't fleas it was trying to get rid of, they were barbarians. And it wasn't scratching, it was fighting.

Apart from a short period in the second century AD, there was always trouble somewhere on the borders of the Empire. No matter how far the Romans advanced, there were always more barbarians beyond the border, barbarians who watched the Empire with greedy eyes. Many of them knew about Roman ways from first hand experience, perhaps having fought as auxiliaries. As the years passed, more and more barbarians were employed as soldiers by the Empire, for instance Saxon soldiers were stationed in Britain to fight off their fellow barbarians.

PICTING A FIGHT

Britain had its fair share of barbarian bust-ups. *Picts* raided across Hadrian's Wall, *Scots* (originally from Ireland) raided the west coast thus avoiding the Wall, and *Saxon* pirates plundered along the east coast as early as the third century. But as long as the Empire was strong it was easy to punish the trouble makers.

It didn't stay strong for ever ...

FOUR REASONS FOR WEAKNESS

1. Romans were never very good at choosing new emperors. More often than not, after one emperor died or was killed there was a civil war before a new emperor won power. They spent more time fighting each other than they did fighting barbarians.

2. Rich Romans behaved liked ostriches with their heads in the sand. They retreated to their luxurious villas in the country and spent less time and money on looking after the towns. They tried to pretend that things could go on as they were for ever.

3. Vast private estates called *latifundia* sprang up all over the Empire. The gap between rich and poor widened into a yawning chasm. Life at the bottom was tough, and to those at the bottom barbarian invasions must often have seemed like a way to escape oppression.

4. Some historians blame the rise of Christianity for the fall of Rome. Christianity was like a mole, burrowing away at the foundations of Roman rule such as Emperor worship and slavery.

Ostriches are said to bury their heads in the sand when in danger, believing that if they can't see the danger it doesn't exist.

5. By the 280s the North Sea was already crawling with Saxon pirates. A Celtic sailor called Carausius was ordered to clear them out. He seems to have been quite successful and several massive naval bases around the south and east coasts of England (the 'Forts of the Saxon Shore') may have been his work. But later he turned to piracy himself, declared himself Emperor and set up an independent empire in Britain for a while.

4. The first warning of more serious trouble came in 342 when the Emperor Constans, one of the sons of Constantine, had to make a hurried visit to Britain to repel barbarian raiders who had crossed over Hadrian's Wall. He beat them back.

3. By the 360s the barbarians were back. Picts, Scots, Attacotti  and Saxons attacked at the same time. Hadrian's Wall and the Forts of the Saxon Shore were overrun. Deserters from the army and escaped slaves joined the barbarians and roamed the land for two years, plundering and killing until order was restored.

2. In AD 409 most of the Roman army withdrew from Britain to fight in Europe. Realizing that their Roman governors had become more of a hindrance than a help, the Britons threw them out of the country and, as the historian Zosimus puts it: 'took up arms, braving danger for their independence and freed their cities of the barbarians ...'

The *Attacotti* were cannibals according to Saint Jerome. They came either from Ireland or the Western Isles.

117

1. By 410 the barbarians were back. The Britons appealed to the Emperor Honorius for help against the Saxons. He wrote back telling them he was unable to help them.

Honorius' letter spelt the end of Roman rule in Britain, after nearly four hundred years. From then on the Romano-Britons had to fend for themselves as best they could.

FINIS

DARK AGES PAGES

Even after four hundred years of Roman rule, the Romano-Britons were still Celts beneath their togas. It seems that as they struggled to survive, they stopped behaving very much like Romans at all. There is evidence that in many places they retreated to their ancient hill-forts for safety. In fact one of the reasons that civilization died in Britain may well be that the ordinary British never cared as much for Roman ways as the Romans thought they did.

Even so, the next hundred and fifty years from AD 400-550 were a nightmare for the Romano-Britons, a nightmare from which they never woke up. They were battered by waves of barbarians from every direction, until at last they drowned in a sea of Saxon invaders and immigrants. Civilization had died in what is known as the *Dark Ages* 🐾 .

🐾 'Dark' because there are very few written records from this time to shed light on what was happening.

119

If a Romano-Britain had returned from the grave a hundred and fifty years after Honorius wrote his letter, he would have had trouble recognizing his country. He would have seen that the villas, which had struggled on in the countryside until around AD 450 or even later were crumbling ruins, as were the great public buildings in the deserted towns (which some Saxons thought were the work of giants).

Perhaps the biggest shock would have been finding that most people spoke a different language. So many immigrants came from Germany that their language, Saxon, became the language of the country. Modern

English is based mainly on early Saxon. We speak the language of the barbarians, not of the defenders.

We speak a language  which comes from the barbarians, but the majority of modern Britons are a mixture of both British and Saxon. It's strange to think that their ancestors were once involved in a savage war with each other.

But that's history for you.

Finis

Although based on Saxon, modern English contains many words taken from Latin at a later date, mostly via French which is based on Latin.

Finis is Latin for 'The End'.

ROMAN RELICS

COULD *YOU* BE A ROMAN? (PART 4)

The Romans really were like giants. Their influence is everywhere - in our language, our laws, our arts and our buildings, even in the weeds in our gardens. It would take several books the size of this one to list a fraction of what we have inherited from them. So which one of the following have we *not* inherited from the Romans?

a   rabbits

b   beer

c   towns ending in ester, cester and chester etc.

d   nettles

e   Saturday

f   French, Spanish, Romanian and Italian languages

g   words ending in 'ion'

h   the months of the year

i   lots of straight roads such as the A5

Saturday was named after the god Saturn

Romans are said to have whipped themselves with nettles for warmth

---

COULD *YOU* BE A ROMAN? - ANSWERS

Score 10 points for each right answer

Part 1	Part 2	Part 3	Part 4
1 b	a 23	c	beer
2 a	b 47		
3 c	c 174		

Less than 30   Useless - go back to barbarism

30+   Not bad - time to take out the toga

60+   First class - lie down for dinner

INDEX

WHAT THEY DON'T TELL YOU ABOUT...

ABOUT THE AUTHOR

Bob Fowke is a prize-winning children's author.
He has written (or co-written) over seventy exciting books,
from history and science to dinosaurs and spaceships.

Bob started off painting book covers for science-fictionand
horror stories by famous writers such as HP Lovecraft and
Philip K Dick.

Bob is now the editorial advisor at www.youcaxton.co.uk - a
company that offers support to Self-Publishers.